Clay Unbreakables A New Mythology for the Homesick

Clay Unbreakables:
A New Mythology for the Homesick

Natalia Andrievskikh

Clay Unbreakables A New Mythology for the Homesick

Contents

Part One

Keepsake / 11

Patience / 12

The War was Yesterday / 13

Summer Alchemy / 14

Taste for Suspense / 15

Home Remedies for the Lovesick / 16

The Dangers of Serendipity / 17

A Pastoral in White / 19

No Room for Visitors / 20

Encounter / 21

Unfortunate Affairs / 22

A Word about Love / 23

The End of an Era / 24

Laws of Gravitation / 25

Part Two

The Tornado Season / 29

You Must Go Back Before You Go Forward / 30

The Unsightly Magic / 31

Small Talk / 32

Quarter of a Tarot Card / 33

The Comfort of Being Prepared / 34

The Fine Art of Doubt / 35

Matters of Consequence / 36

As Seen Through the Keyhole / 37

When Time Gets the Best of You / 38

A Failed Attempt at Damage Control / 39

An Equation with All Unknowns / 40

A Vignette for the Soul / 41

Narcissus Revisited / 42

Something Else Entirely / 43

Part Three

Diary of a Bluestocking / 47

Clay Unbreakables / 48

Happy Approximation / 50

Just Another Day / 52

Snowed In / 54

Those Worlds Outside Your Door / 55

Ways of the World / 56

The Geometry of Pleasure / 57

Down the Slippery Road / 58

Alive / 59

That Simple / 60

A Game Against Time / 61

What You Fear the Most Cannot Happen / 62

All Good Things Come in Threes / 63

Clay Unbreakables A New Mythology for the Homesick

PART ONE

Clay Unbreakables A New Mythology for the Homesick

KEEPSAKE

When I say good-bye I sing old travel songs. They say, go, stranger, leave with a light heart, I have yet more to give. But they are not too many; with this last one gone, I am voiceless.

Don't you worry though; I will not let you go empty-handed. Take my silver rings still warm from my skin. Tear away patches from my sleeves, hems of my skirt; take my hairpins, coils of my hair, my humpty-dumpty wrists and joints and ribs. Snap off my fingers made of sugar: I don't want you to be hungry on the road. Strip me down of feathers, pull off my snake skin, its ornaments getting dull. Pack it all in small boxes to keep on the bottom of your travel bag, little trifles of eyelashes and fingerprints and bits of the collar bone. Put them away. Don't count the pieces.

In the empty room, a piano is playing. The sounds are heaping up and crumbling, falling down with a rattle, scattering like raindrops, like buttons, like pearls. In the old speckled mirror, you can see them pouring down. It smells of mothballs and burnt candles.

PATIENCE

When they say loss it sounds round and empty like an ugly coin. I didn't lose anything, I carry it all with me on my back. At times it becomes a snail house and I hide in it, cuddling among old knitted cardigans and balls of yarn. Or it turns into sinewy wings and I am this huge moth falling into the sky, sprinkling silver dust all around. My throat stuffed with happiness.

It happens when I remember, but I mostly don't. I remembered yesterday, and the day before that, but not anymore, so I walk around counting the city corners. The streets murmur it to me in husky voices, and echo bounces it back from moving cars and buses. Store windows swing signs at me, and trees follow me with a thousand worried eyes.

I sit down on a bench while the day is melting away, fresh secrets getting old. I think about kissing the trees on the warm eyes, drinking their green breath. The sky is slowly rolling over, its other side heavy with ripe colors of the evening.

THE WAR WAS YESTERDAY

Out in the woods, my grandmother is a little girl kneeling to drink from a deep groove in the forest road left by a cart. Her feet are wrapped in straps of cloth. It is late summer, and they have already taken away the older boys to load trains with guns at the station where they sleep for two hours a day on wooden boxes of bullets. They have already taken away old Aunt Ksenia for stealing from the field a handful of wheat grains for the little ones. But it is still summer, the sunflower stalks are meaty and mint and chamomile boiled with rainwater soothe the aching bowels. Last winter, their schoolteacher was found chewed to bone on her way to school one morning; she had run out of paper to burn to scare away the wolves. But it is still summer, the sun falls down through tree branches in curly shades and the narrow road runs far out of the woods into a sunny pastoral. My grandmother drinks greedily; the rains taste of milk shores and sweet syrup.

SUMMER ALCHEMY

Do you remember the heavy, watery smell of saltbush behind the old shed where we used to play hide-and-seek for hours, staring at the rotting planks of wood? Tucked in all shades of silence, one-on-one with the invisible lives of rusty nails, buttons and broken glass dug out from the ground, dolls made of grass – they were beautiful, too, with hair long as mountain rivers, their green bosoms soft and quivering. As the day would grow old, the wooden shed grunting on its chicken legs, we'd forget we were hiding until our stomachs reminded us to climb out of the saltbush – but the smell of it, heated up by the sun, do you remember this smell? I am constantly brought back to it in my travels, as I am climbing up the narrow stone-paved streets and see the neighborhood children running around with fried bread and tree twigs in their hands. Oh, the stories I could tell them! But I walk past them into my room, open the window into the stuffy southern night, and wish the river dolls sweet dreams; and then the quietest of them all, the ox-eyed princess, braids my hair as I am falling asleep.

TASTE FOR SUSPENSE

If you are bored, go talk to the old fisherman who lives right next to the river in a small house of grey wood, its window the size of a pocket. He will wink at you from under his bushy eyebrows bleached by the sun and tell about today's catch. There he is, gutting the fish and talking to himself while the gypsy boys squat nearby, waiting. He does not keep his haul; the boys pick it up and sell it on the roadside to passing cars. Instead, he keeps whatever he finds inside the glistening fish bellies: buttons, safety pins, pebbles, hooks, rings; he will show you, you won't even have to ask. Running out of time here, he'll say, opening the box where he stores his trove, so little time and so much more to discover. He found a whole pinky once inside a large sad-looking carp. He cleaned it from the fish guts and let it dry out in the sun.

HOME REMEDIES FOR THE LOVESICK

Gingerbread stars and a jar of milk in the deep grass by the river. I am keeping that night in my herbarium of dried souls. Without you there, I was a white stone basking in the roaring orchestra of colors until they hushed away, overcast by the indigo vertebrae of the night. A warm enchanted stone, white as the milk in the jar, as starlight on the skin of water. Had you kissed me, the warmth would have stayed on your lips, the gingerbread spice melting against your palate. Had you kissed me, the river would have stirred and startled the dragonflies slumbering in the bulrush. But something had held you back, and I watched the darkness tarry around in circles, then grow shy and numb, then surrender. I walked away with a needle in my heart, brimming over with prickly light, diluted smells of ground wet before the dawn, the river folk murmur and rattle.

THE DANGERS OF SERENDIPITY

She is lying on the floor in the corner, the blanket stuffed with geese feathers is itchy and smells of dust. It is not as hot here on the floor; the corner is even a little damp, the wooden logs tarnished with time. But she can still feel the heat outside, acacia and sagebrush drying out in the sun, vapors from the river clotting in the air. A storm is coming soon from behind the corner of the horizon, but they don't know it yet, only she does. She always knows. She can hear the others chuckling and arguing in the kitchen, doors screeching, knives tapping against the cutting board. Just wait, they will know soon, too. Fried onion and fresh chopped dill, wild mushrooms they are cleaning from dirt and leaves. The outhouse stench, oils and spirits from the medicine cabinet, camphor-balls in the wardrobe. The clatter of pans and dishes, the cat yawping for food, flies buzzing, and yes, here it comes – burry thunder, hurried steps, sharp voices of the girls gathering the laundry from the line to save it from getting soaked again. The first wet beads of dust on the road, dogs upset at the wind, the oozy smell, the purple curtain of water, the pain and the beauty of it all.

And then, when this all ends, when the headache melts into a thin soap bubble and vanishes, the world will burst open and silent. She will walk across the room, her knees numb and tingling, and open the window into the deafening light, the clear contours of the trees, tanned children playing in the mud with red plastic buckets, the air washed crisp and clean like a faceted glass. And she will be grateful and hungry.

A PASTORAL IN WHITE

The break for lunch in the provincial hospital is quieter than usual, and not only because it's Wednesday and the busiest times fall on Mondays and Fridays. A bus with foreign tourists turned over on the highway next to the town a couple of days ago, so most of the hospital personnel is in the new wing looking busy, while here in the main building they stopped taking walk-ins after the first patch of patients early in the morning.

Lisa, the young janitor, is washing the floors for the second time today, which is already more than a whole week's standard. She has sneaked into the new wing to hunt for signatures: she wanted to ask if it's true that the streets abroad are paved with yellow stones and palm trees grow on every corner. The thing is, she did not know how to explain herself, so she poked the patients with the end of her broom and finally got kicked out. She is bored now and peeks into the keyhole of the dentist's, where the doctor, a middle-aged divorcee with henna-burnt hair, is leisurely drilling her own tooth without anesthesia, looking at herself in a pocket mirror. The crack in the window behind her as a crooked line of blue scotch tape.

NO ROOM FOR VISITORS

The kettle is on in her little kitchen 4x2.5 women's square steps. The table is covered with a plastic plaid table cloth that expatriates in France call Eastern European. It makes them feel nostalgic and teary.

The last time the floor was cleaned was when the tooth fairy came to her son who is now a long-distance truck driver and sends her articles on agriculture cut from local newspapers from the places he stays overnight. That's his way of asking about his father, of whom he only has vague agricultural associations, probably because of a story she once told him and forgot. She is good with stories: she teaches drama at high school, and sometimes stays late for the theater club, sneaking out during breaks to buy cigarettes from the newspaper kiosk at the bus stop while her students argue over their roles.

What they don't know is how bored she gets spellchecking the scripts on weekends in her kitchen, the kettle on and the windows open into spring where poplar trees spit white cotton all over. Inside, it smells of ammonia and old books, and the beetroot juice she uses for ink like her grandmother did in war time dries out quickly, as she smokes with her favorite cat, composing letters to her son that she never sends.

ENCOUNTER

A young girl throwing up behind a pretentious local restaurant called London-Pub. Back in the days, they say, the building used to be a stable. Now, the outside stank of city juice. Since there was nobody there to hold up her long hair the color of straw, she clung to the wooden wall of the building with only one hand, her sharp elbow rising above her head like a unicorn's horn.

She paused to breathe rhythmically, scrutinizing the ground under her feet peppered with earthworms after last night's rain. A solemn-looking toad the size of a bulldog appeared on her right, picking up the worms with his quick ribbon tongue. They looked into each other's eyes for a long heavy moment, breathing in from two opposite sides the damp air that stuck to the nostrils.

In the street in front of the restaurant, the girl's friends shouted her name and something about getting a taxi. Have you called her cell; she must have left with that bearded moron who sent a bottle to our table. I should probably go, the girl said, her voice making a sound of foam rubber against glass. The toad nodded with understanding.

UNFORTUNATE AFFAIRS

At thirty-two, he still had all of his milk teeth. They looked great, too, luminous, orderly rows of little buttons. He showed them off on the first pages of local weeklies until a Hungarian diva desired them for a necklace. "I've heard it is your custom, she said, to show generosity of spirit and hospitality." He bowed and dropped a glance at her cleavage.

You can find him selling fried chestnuts on the side streets these days. If you think it is easy to sell your soul, go talk to him first; he knows better. A soul likes to be stolen, he says with a lisp, offering you a taste. Listen to him; he will tell you about love and great opera, and how to roast memories on a turnspit until they glisten with golden crust.

A WORD ABOUT LOVE

In this parade of eccentrics, my uncle is still the odd one out. He died long ago but is still keeping a paramour ballerina in a snuffbox. He visits her every night as a ghost and they carry on long conversations about Stravinsky or the latest oil crisis. Music and money are always in fashion. My aunt listens to them from the other room but has no interest in parlor talk. Damn anorexics, she mumbles and heads to the kitchen. When uncle leaves she tries to feed the ballerina butter on toast. Come morning the bread is gone and the ballerina as lovely and still as she's ever been.

THE END OF AN ERA

This is where we part ways, even if it means that I will never quite feel at home any more. Waking up in a new place every morning, fancy that. Coffee and pastries in cafes that look vaguely familiar, statues that wink at you the moment you turn away, so you have to pinch your elbow and clear your throat. The way waiters smile at you is always slightly indecent, just enough to tickle the butterflies in your ribcage on your way out; doors opening into daylight; archways lined with eggshells; faces, voices, humming of crowded streets, always new, always the same.

It feels strange to be the one leaving, not the one left behind this time; strange and exciting and wrong, but inevitable, and comforting because of that. I know I'll be looking for the old city between the lines, in the gaps between buildings, behind the corners of fruit stalls and flower shops. The postcards I send back always picture doors – green doors, red doors, locked doors, wooden doors, doors decorated with brass doorknobs and horseshoes, doors so seductively closed – and one of them, at least one, I know, opens all the way through to the other side, where it has just rained, and the air smells of the morning sky above the cobblestone alleyways, above the gray rooftops, above the small airport on the fringe of a birch tree grove.

LAWS OF GRAVITATION

At take-off, the stewardess recites emergency instructions in unbearably bad English. The passengers are scared dolls, thin threads stick out of their sleeves, stretching out of the plane and beyond the landing strips, back to the gaudy furniture and narrow kitchen tables on the second, fifth and ninth floors of red- bricked apartment blocks. With the plane gathering height, the threads stretch and become thinner like strings of melted mozzarella.

Nobody knows why the young man in stylish glasses keeps asking for more pink napkins, cramps and twists them into weird shapes. The elderly lady in the seat next to him thinks he is nervous and pats him on the hand, her knotted fingers wedged apart with too many gold rings. The stewardess is just angry with him because he drops the used napkins on the floor under his seat.

When the mozzarella strings reach their breaking point he finally twists a napkin into a flower shape to give to the blonde girl who sleeps in her seat across the aisle, an open long-lashed eye painted with watercolors in the center of her forehead.

Clay Unbreakables A New Mythology for the Homesick

PART TWO

Clay Unbreakables A New Mythology for the Homesick

THE TORNADO SEASON

The sides of the world are many, but you only know it when they all mix up and crash and pile up on you, and you can't breathe because you are just gulping in sand which scratches your throat and you cannot hear what's inside your own head because of all the ringing and squealing and clatter. I could not see the sky anymore from the little tree house I was hiding in; I did not even know where the sky was. What I saw I did not have time to name because it disappeared right away. I saw my brother moving funny through the air with his mouth open. I saw a barrel from our neighbor's backyard hitting him from behind. No wonder he got really scared then, so scared he turned into a little shivering puppy when I finally caught him by the paw. I must have twisted it out of socket because he was whimpering as I pulled him inside and locked the latch behind us. Don't you worry, I said, looking into his puppy eyes, it's gonna be okay. See, we are flying, I said, we are inside the Jinni's long twirling beard, just as you said we would be; remember, you always wanted to see it close by, so here, here.

YOU MUST GO BACK BEFORE YOU GO FORWARD

The old crone laughs at the tea leaves on the bottom of my cup. Oh my, she says; what a delight! But you must forgive me; I haven't laughed like this in a thousand years. I nod obediently, while she scratches the back of her head with the looking- glass handle. I beg your pardon, I offer, but she is already talking to an elderly gentleman in a checkered beret. He sweats from under his glasses and she licks her lips, tapping her nails with chipped polish on the windowsill.

THE UNSIGHTLY MAGIC

The learned crow wets a pencil with spit and readjusts another border. On the butchered map, history is waving flags and chanting obscenities. A half-colored movie, shots flickering. Now, a giant toddler steps on the house of cards, the crowd by its feet oblivious and hungry. The next moment, you see a peasant carrying a bunny by its ears. Every minute, a street lamp dies, the beads of night lights count uneven.

What you don't know is that the eyelets have all been sewn tight. The calendar has already ended; they are dreaming your dreams and counting the notches on your nose. Sit back and enjoy the show.

SMALL TALK

My geranium is watching me. From around the corner, the worries of tomorrow protrude their snouts in a hungry gesture. And, trust me on this, if you look closely, you will see the chief joker masquerading as a museum guide. *Love*, he says, *freedom, tartar sauce*, waving at you with a pointer.

They are right to be wary of me: I know that the ways to lose heart run the gamut. We are all entries in the stockpile of forbidden dreams. We don't know the names that they have for us; we do not even know what we are capable of.

QUARTER OF A TAROT CARD

A paper square tossed around by the wind, all the answers missing. What remains is a hint of a shoulder, a fractured hand holding a ribbon. Is it the sad Arlecchino who has just slipped in the middle of a high-wire act, his invisible violin smashed into flinders? Or the Raven, dispossessed of his feathers, nesting for the night in the shadow of the church bell? Or maybe it is the Muse with her ribs broken, howling in the scrap-heap. An old lady walks up to her with a limp, feeds her yesterday's soup, bread soaked in sour milk. What happens next is not a sight for the squeamish. You guess, you swipe a tear, you look away.

Clay Unbreakables A New Mythology for the Homesick

THE COMFORT OF BEING PREPARED

Let me tell you, we got it all wrong. The world is flat and it floats in the sea of cuckoo's tears. A sad toad that sits at its edge unlocks its jaws and swallows planes whole. They broadcast it all on the radio, but nobody listens; people are busy taking sleep aid or rummaging yard sales.

I would know; I was a priest's betrothed in a past life. He always kept an eye on the horizon and spoke in codes. "It looks like rain," he'd say, but what he meant was, "The judgment day is close." I would sit quietly next to him and listen to the toad's stomach rumbling. Every now and then, a doll's limb from a lost plane would fall out of the sky and land in our rice pudding.

THE FINE LINE OF DOUBT

I wonder if it's true that nothing ever ends entirely, but keeps going on somewhere, in a parallel universe, in a wooden photo frame, in a dusty diary tucked away on the shelf between Proust and Tolstoy. If it's true, and it might as well be, then I am scared, out of my mind scared about tomorrow, because what this means is there can be nothing new, nothing unmarred and austere, but a chain of familiar ghosts knocking on the door in the midst of my spring insomnia, asking for attention. If I only knew what to say to be entertaining! But I'm a nuisance at conversation, with too many questions to ask. What do we really need to know about our origins? Why does knowing where we come from weigh us down; and how come that not knowing is the only thing worse than that? And – please allow me this last one – if I try hard enough to forget, will I un-see the arrow of my lifeline, always pointing back to the base of the palm?

In a spring of too many ghosts, it is hard to breathe. As the evening gets closer, I am making some tea, glancing at the mirror to practice polite chit-chat. My cat dismisses the whole thing with snobbish indifference. He is getting old and spends more time sleeping these days, dreaming of those distant worlds that only cats can go to in their sleep.

MATTERS OF CONSEQUENCE

Last night, I rescued Gogol from a small curiosity shop on the corner. He smelled of lavender and chewing tobacco and was missing one ear, but his eyes were sharp as in the olden days before he was buried alive, tucked in red velvet. Have you heard, I told him, they started putting cell phones into fresh graves and have already saved eighteen people! *Enchanté*, he replied, his accent thick with dust.

The woman that wrapped him in tissue paper did not like me, I could tell; she kept knocking on the wood counter and spitting behind her shoulder. Who knows, I must have broken some sacred unwritten rules of her universe and am now banished indeterminably, the way I do not trust people who don't like chocolate.

AS SEEN THROUGH THE KEYHOLE

The white-washed sky leans on the granite banisters like a huge plastic lid, the lonely plazas stand torpid from the night. In this part of the world, endless days grow into one another without the interruption of sunset. The gutted springs of the cuckoo clock swing their long tongues, the paint is peeling on the window-sill from too much contact with elbows, and the insomniac Yannis who lives under my pillow dips her feet in the whisky, kicks the ice cube with her big toe and asks for a kiss.

Oh, she should know better than that; she spends her nights tickling me with her painted nails, tugging me by the nose, entangling me with curvy loops until I am stiff and helpless. And then how slowly she munches on my limbs, chewy like gummy-bears, her eyes closed in pleasure! I wait and count the sheep running through the granite streets, swinging on the clock springs, bleating along the grey bridges. In her dream, she makes me doubt myself. As the sky lid gets heavier, I am waiting for her to stop gnawing on my bones as she dozes off… but she gets dangerously closer each time, she used to wake up much earlier before; I am afraid that once she will just keep on sleeping until it is too late. She dreams me up in her sleep, she dreams me out of my skin, and I nudge her to stop and look me in the eye – just look me in the eye, let me be, I am tired, so tired of counting sheep.

WHEN TIME GETS THE BEST OF YOU

At the congress of runaway clock hands, you are a chance onlooker. In the Grand Ballroom, wasp waitresses with golden wings serve champagne to the delegates as you are watching through the doorway, beaming with pleasure. O, the splendor of forgetting, the swooning joy of having lost both of your birth names! The hourglass lady at the reception desk looks disapprovingly, wonders if she can help you. You ask for a map of the city, and she brings you half of a newspaper stamped with coffee mug circles. Never mind, sweetheart, I was just leaving; in the patina of these hallways, it is so easy to get distracted.

The door shuts behind you with a round click. Outside, street boys are playing Frisbee with an orphaned clock face. To both sides of you, the city rolls itself up in red brick.

A FAILED ATTEMPT AT DAMAGE CONTROL

We are only afraid of what we don't know, so I picture all the dead ends and closed doors I can fathom to break free of fear. A waiting room where we are stuck forever, listening to the news on repeat, with toy cups of unreasonably bad coffee and old crackers from the bottom of our pockets. Freight trains halfway sunk in the swamp, stuffed with rusty nails from top to bottom. A city fenced off by the *papier-mâché* wall of sea, where they serve stale éclairs and lemonade on a terrace with white plastic tables, while the accordion is playing the same morbidly upbeat song for eternity. That one false note keeps scratching my ear. I pick at the wall with clay fingers, and black night clots under my fingernails. Some day it will give in and crumble, unclench the ossified jaws of the in-between. Until then, I stay put, keep the fingers of my free hand crossed behind my back.

AN EQUATION WITH ALL UNKNOWNS

You take a picture of me and I freeze like a speck of a pine nut shell in amber, my arms above my head and my hair scattered in the wind. Kayapos believe that when your photo is taken, a part of your soul is forever trapped in the image, and I imagine myself peeling off, splitting into a billion thin layers that follow me like a trail. I think of the loose cells of hair and nail dust that I leave behind everywhere I go. If I spit on the ground, will I walk away from myself? Have I planted parts of my soul in the strangest places, park benches half the world from here, old city trains covered in too much graffiti, on the background of somebody's tourist shots soaking in the developing tray? And, when I inhabit a strange skin and can no longer remember my name, will I still be me, every bit as much as this girl in your picture laughing in the wind, blissfully unafraid to lose her freckles to the disintegrating meat of time?

A VIGNETTE FOR THE SOUL

If I dream of floods so often, it is because I cannot swim, and the thought of losing your hand under water terrifies me. That I might wake up one day and be one more beautiful lost thing among those beautiful lost things under the weight of memory, what an exquisite nightmare. Those underwater worlds, with their plangent corridors lined with slimy yellow moss, where I saw a pale banshee drinking tea with a catfish once, her tinsel fingers trembling as she sobbed. Is it her eyes that make sea salt? I can't tell. Where seahorses dance their courtship, under that tilted stone, I will be waiting for you, hoping that you will reach out for me in your sleep and click me awake one moment before my throat fills with water.

NARCISSUS REVISITED

And then the story fails you, but that is perhaps inevitable, given the heat and the limited number of signifiers. And how can you tell about this embroidery of sounds, moaning of invisible creatures and the plaintive call from the towers, seagulls laughing at you at night from the bay, choking with laughter at your attempts to write it all down? The impossible white and blue of the water and the domes scattered on the opposite shore, on the anthill of little windows and roofs faded from the sun. The story of a girl crying for the flower she dreamt of, which is not a story at all, but the first and stinging discovery of beauty. You reach out for it, stubborn tears hot in your mouth, and it is red, or perhaps even a brighter color, and they say you have to walk for it until your feet burn, but it is still too far away. Maybe there are pathways carved up its bright flesh to the core which smells of honey fields and dew. Maybe the road to it is paved with broken words and bubbling sobs, with monstrous angles and circles from a feverish dream. The story stops at this point, but the flower never stops staining the retina with beauty. Everything else may fail you, but the flower never will, even if you have to dream it up anew every time, the pattern of its veins and petals, the burning of its mane in the distance.

SOMETHING ELSE ENTIRELY

I am taking care of my fear. Greeting him at the door with a kiss, cradling his sharp shoulders like a bundled-up snow statue. In the noose of my arms, he grows frail by the hour; so thin he can hide behind the loose seams in the wall-paper, squeeze into windowsill cracks. I leave out breadcrumbs and sweets by the window: valiant as I am, I am no murderer. What else can I say in my defense? That love is a two-syllable word; you drop one from your lips, you keep the other hidden deep under your breastbone. That I have never been happier than right now, in this very moment, falling into the night with the darkness on the other side of the bed carved in your image, when you are playing my echo on the opposite end of the world, both of our throats slit by the same delirious blade.

Clay Unbreakables A New Mythology for the Homesick

PART THREE

Clay Unbreakables A New Mythology for the Homesick

DIARY OF A BLUESTOCKING

I am getting ready for a siege. In my attic, where I hide from reason, there is enough light and dry chamomile to make tea to last me a lifetime, or at least until Monday. I am wearing bones of a jaybird in a silk sachet around my neck, a full set, to keep me company: I have learned to trust the invisible. As the evening sets in, I watch dust grains tumbling in the sunrays, stopping the show at the grand theater of secret ambitions. Bones and words, dust and tears: a world in the making in which you take no part. Life is a string of first lines falling in mid-air never to be picked up again, I know that much; that is why I've been packing them tight in my heart, far from the connoisseurs of embroidered language. Always craving for more.

They will catch up with me, of course; I have no doubt. But before they break in and ransack my pockets, I will assemble the bird bones with my breath, and the jay will shake up and take wing, the attic behind her empty and brushed up with muddled colors of the evening.

CLAY UNBREAKABLES

Back there, I had a twin sister who knew my every thought and looked pretty even when she had just woken up. We had so much fun masking the black circles under our eyes that were not there, it was hilarious, kill the crocodiles, we would say, we are killing the crocodiles. Creating some beautiful Lolitas.

She took me with her on the night bus around the city; after eight the bus changed from number 5 to 15 and then to 47, and we stayed on until we were motion sick and the night was navy blue oil on canvas. The moon is a hole from somebody's point finger, she said, but if you want to prick the sky through with your finger all the way to the other side, you need to know how to fly. She did not have to say that, I knew it already, and she knew I knew it, and she knew I would fly and she would not because she wouldn't have to. She also knew it was fun to eat crushed warm strawberries together out of a plastic bag, brushing the sticky red across the face like a crooked smile. I thought of kissing her on the blood-red mouth when she laughed like that. But then she started liking beer too much, and beer kills the aftertaste of strawberries.

I flew away on a moonless night counting to a hundred and backwards not to be afraid. The night looked more like a gray cold cardboard box outside the round window two rows away from the lavatory, where the air was sucking in toilet seats and spitting them out into the sky.

HAPPY APPROXIMATION

I wake up into the middle of a story, into all this humming and laughter and hurrying some place that I've never heard of. But no, you say, of course you've seen it before, remember, when you were trying to teach me to waltz? That's right, you are there, too, with these awkward brown elbow patches, your hair is longer and all messed up by the wind, and we just can't stop talking, we talk, and laugh, and I breathe hard from running, because you always walk so fast that I have to run next to you. You know the way well, I'd get lost here by myself in these stairways, a riverwalk half-flooded with melting snow; we pass by a flock of boats all bundled up in blue plastic, but not cold at all. I see Gigi walking towards us, how you look at her; she is just back from modeling and the smear of rouge on her face is even brighter against her pale neck. You guys had to see this, she says; she is hysterical as I take her furs off, my eyes glued to the white of her skin. We are walking there on that damn red carpet, she says, and I look down and there are roaches everywhere under our feet, they crunch as I step on them. And those damn lights straight in my face, she says and starts crying, hot and salty, and your hands are on her neck, your long fingers. I pull at your hand, but my eyes are closing, the roaches splatter across the red carpet and down the endless staircases, and I am falling asleep, sinking into your muffled voice, her flowery smell, the sobbing and the patter.

JUST ANOTHER DAY

When the train disappeared from sight, she suddenly felt light and almost happy. Done, it was done; it didn't matter anymore after all. Her body, too, did not matter, or did not exist, at least not in the same shape as before. It was somehow stretchable, scattered all over the triangle streets, the paper lanterns, the flocks of yachts swinging in the fold. She could see the bend of her own neck in the arch across the road, a side of her hip in the round office building to the left of a little city park. It must have been a holiday of some sort because there were people everywhere, floating out of the park and from the streets behind it, dressed in bright hats with feathers; they were eating ice-cream and dropping colorful wraps on the ground. She bought an ice-cream cone, too, from a street vendor wearing green elephant ears, and gave him a wink.

Down the street, the raw warm smell of baking bread hugged her, and she ran forward, cutting right through trees, benches, passers-by. It felt like flying down on the swings, when the wind is loud in the ears and it gets very cold in the pit of the stomach. When she stopped, the street was not crowded anymore, only an old woman with a curly-haired little boy were sitting on the side of the road, cracking sunflower seeds. She sat down next to them and stretched her legs; dusty sandals, skirt above the knees, a fading bruise on the left ankle. As their eyes met, the curly-haired boy smiled at her and came closer; she saw his lips moving, muttering something inaudible. She smiled back. The boy touched her face with both his hands and started pecking freckles off her skin with fast, short pinches.

SNOWED IN

The door is blocked from the outside, so she climbs out of the window. Lingers on the roof for just a moment, but it's not high at all anymore, the snow pile rising almost up to the roof. She slides down right into the crunching snow up to the shoulders, flops about, crawls outside. She is all white now, even the black woolen socks. The boots are stuck back inside the snow mountain.

A cake, she thinks, an ice-cream cake with whipped cream and condensed milk and coconut powder. People are shoveling their way through the cake with big spoons, mouthfuls of fresh crispiness. Narrow tunnels run crookedly from house to house, from one rim of the giant cake to the other.

She walks through the park, dipping her legs knee high; a loose end of her untied scarf drags along after her. She looks up, trying to see what is happening there behind the fluffy blur. Sky children are playing pillow fight, white stuffing flying all over.

THOSE WORLDS OUTSIDE YOU DOOR

They all left for a walk, carrying high-pitched cries and dolls with blinking eyes out into the yard. The curly-haired kid stayed in his bed pretending to sleep, watching a fat fly travel across his blanket. He had just wet the sheets and was pondering a confession since it didn't look like he could just pretend it didn't happen.

As nobody came up to check on him, he grew annoyed at what the others must be doing out there with his favorite red-wheeled truck. The truck was what he regretted giving up the most. The nurse behind the door was talking over the phone in a shrill complaining voice, telling somebody to fry the potatoes, no, don't use that knife, too sharp, take out the pre-cut potatoes from the freezer, and for God's sake, please, please turn down the music, I cannot hear you. She hung up and peeked into the empty room with a chain of smelly footprints leading out into the sun, voices bubbling outside in the crisp midday air.

WAYS OF THE WORLD

She arrives at a small town by the seaside, unchaperoned, her eyes gleaming and her lips painted bright red. The old man at the reception desk asks to see her ID before checking her in, but she laughs and smudges his cheekbone with a peck; of course she is not traveling by herself, could he be a dear and keep her luggage for a short while? It is high tide and the water is close, and her feet hurt so awfully, awfully much after the road. He obliges, or rather, he has no time to respond before she is out of the door, the room behind her translucent and jammed with too much space.

Down by the water, she kicks her sandals aside and tucks up her skirt. A boy playing with pebbles in the shadow of his mother's pink parasol wishes she had a ball that he could fetch if it gets blown away by the wind. He squeezes a pebble, forgetting to unclench his clammy fist, and the hot stone burns through to the back of his hand. He watches as she climbs on top of a rock and starts picking at a blister on her foot with a twig. The air is so clear that one can see feathers on the wings of seagulls hovering over the sleek skin of the sea, as well as the scared eyes of the fish that they snatch out of water with sharp, nimble beaks.

THE GEOMETRY OF PLEASURE

The universe is expanding and tomorrow it will take me longer to walk to your house, a book in my left hand and a bunch of daisies in the right. Nonsense, you will say and shrug your shoulders; of course it would be interesting if it were, but what nonsense. You will shove the book in the stack of paperbacks under the table and perch on the windowsill, plucking the daisies. I will sit down on the floor next to you and watch the opposite wall backing off, the lint balls in between the wardrobe and the mirror growing into objects and piling up on the floor. The radiator will fluff up its ridge like a scared kitten, but you won't notice, far away in your thoughts, moving your lips as you tear apart petal after white petal.

DOWN THE SLIPPERY ROAD

When the world comes undone, he will be walking barefoot on a cobblestone street far away from here or sitting on the grass having lunch, because what can be better than eating a big white juicy apple under the Eiffel tower if there is no tomorrow. He will nibble on the pulp and then pick out all the seeds because they are rich in iodine, and watch how the horizon knits itself out stitch by stitch. He won't even be afraid, well, maybe just a tiny bit, but the thought of the little reed- pipe in his left pocket will make him smile. The scared passers-by will stare at him at a loss and hurry on, and only one little girl will turn her head to see him take a swing and throw the apple core right over the brink.

ALIVE

I was casually boasting about my man's arms when she looked up and said, you know, this is all great of course, but just imagine – it is hot in the sun, the air itself is blurry and shines like amber, and your bones are melting slowly – and you stretch out your body in all its height and run, and then jump, plunge into the water and close your eyes, feel your eyes hot under the eyelids, feel the heat inside you and how every cell of your skin is bursting with pleasure – I would give up all the men in the world for a moment like this.

And her eyes were young and blue like water on a hot summer afternoon.

THAT SIMPLE

One day I will tell Gigi about this all, and she will jump and clap her hands, ticklish with excitement. I will say, you know, Gigi, it was like… no, it felt as if… as if you went apple picking in August and brought home a whole bucket, and you stuck bunches of peppermint leaves and clover between the apples. And it is afternoon and you are tired, just a little, and you decide to close your eyes for a little minute; so you are sleeping and the apples are under the table next to your bed, and they smell, you can feel them smell in your sleep. Tart August sun and winds from the river; that's what it was like, Gigi, you know. And she will say, yeah, I know, and nod, and smile.

A GAME AGAINST TIME

Lilac, a five-petal star, luck hidden somewhere among the dull four-petal clones. Everything is a sign directed at me, the world speaks in wild tongues of a place to build sand castles and cover the parapets with carved stone. Where watermelon juice washes down dust of the aging day. Where I close my eyes and listen to the well telling stories in the orchard, clothed in the thick smell of wet grass and branches heavy with bloom, bunches of straw set aside for a nest. Where it all comes from. I press my warm lips to the chins of tulips, my flower breath coming back with the wonder of open eyes. Where the woodpecker startles me, drowsy and full, and makes my stomach somersault as if when driving very fast up and down a hill. The rolling roulade is swirling in the trees, stirring and beating and fluttering through the air, throbbing from inside me, from under my ribs, up into the throat and into the eyes, itching and burning and blending the four sides of the world in a watercolor swirl.

WHAT YOU FEAR THE MOST CANNOT HAPPEN

I am a knot of branches with twisted emaciated wrists. My toes long and black, digging into the dry dust. I couldn't possibly tell you what's wrong, all is quiet and calm around but for that woman sifting sandflour between her fingers, whispering tales from her memory. A teaspoon of this, a handful of that. An ancient curse that stiffens the springs, turns water into a gray crust on the bottom. The wooden ladle she stirs her tales with has a burnt handle. Her words are stitches pinning me down to one place, hauling my nails deeper into the ground, yellow glassy eyes of nightmare birds that watch me without a blink. The birds curl their claws around my bones, coughing and shifting their weight, wait for a treat. Black scribbles on a transparent canvas. To the left, a road meanders sideways, hard grooves cut through the petrified dirt. I keep an eye on it, my eyelids half closed.

ALL GOOD THINGS COME IN THREES

Where it all comes from, whether it is possible to doubt at all. I am digging my nails in the lifeline, counting summer mornings smashed against the enamel palate of the sky. Hold your breath: it is one moment before the day explodes with car heat, mingling of bodies on the sidewalks, kids' laughter at the squeal of rusty backyard swings. One moment before the city walls bloom with sounds bouncing back into the streets like soccer balls, with rays of rapid yellow from the half-open windows licking my shoulders. The sharp street corners stand wrapped in bakery smells, vapor silhouettes rise from the heated asphalt through the thick breath of maple trees.

Waiting for life to happen.

My own myth of origins, garlands of impossible light weighing me down. Don't hurt me, don't crush these walls like a waxed paper cone. I cannot let go. I know what dreams are worth: I've seen the black in the corner of my eye. In this havoc, the heat thickens colors. The woodpecker's drill is a desperate avalanche of sound coming down in startling waves, washing away time, and I am screaming, squeezing my fists around the flesh-cutting thread that I cling to, that I won't stop clinging to. It's the don't stop-to-breathe kind of mad, it's the hurt-yourself-to-know-you-are-alive kind of mad. The salt on my tongue tastes of the dew on the brims of that old moss-covered well, and I close my eyes and drink, gulp the cold water rising from a black underground belly.

ACKNOWLEDGEMENTS:

The Unsightly Magic; Geometry of Pleasure; Diary of a Bluestocking: forthcoming in Modern Language Studies, Summer Issue, 2016. Print.

The World's Shortest Mystery Novel: Thrice Fiction, Issue 12, 2014. Web and print. Encounter: S/tick, Issue 2.3, 2014. Web.

Laws of Gravitation: Santa Fe Literary Review, 2014. Web and print.

Dangers of Serendipity: Belleville Park Pages, Page 17, March 2014. Print.

Keepsake, Patience, As Seen through the Keyhole, No Room for Visitors, Just Another Day: Connotation Press, September 2013. Web.

That Simple: Graze, Fall 2013. Print.

Down the Slippery Road, Conspiracy Theory, View from the Tower: Yellow Medicine Review, Spring 2013. Print.

A Game Against Time I and II: Rose Red Review, Spring 2013. Web.

The War was Yesterday: Graze, Spring 2013. Print.

Alive: 100 word Story, 2012. Web.

Clay Unbreakables A New Mythology for the Homesick

www.ingramcontent.com/pod-product-compliance
Lightning Source LLC
Chambersburg PA
CBHW030458010526
44118CB00011B/989